Love Is Salvation

Jen Selinsky

Kindle Direct Publishing

ISBN 9798648806108

*Not every poem included in this book is dated in chronological order. This is not an oversight on my part. Rather, I have made changes and substitutions over the years.

-J.L.S.

I made it thru all thanks to you

And the good that

You have done.

Now that may heart is won,

We have nothing to do

But celebrate all the good things

That have blessed our lives

And made them rich to

Combine us into one.

I want to run to you so that

I can hold you in my arms

And never let (you) go!

Tell me you can see all

The wonders that I am

Trying to portray; you are

The light of the day that

Breaks forth at a moment's notice,

My sweet love nested here.

*dedicated to Travis Potts

1/3/06

Whirlwind romance,

We will never have this problem

Because we do not prescribe

To this kind of song and dance.

What others find important,

We think it's obsolete.

I don't need them telling me

That a certain thing will

Make me complete.

We know what we have, and

All that is fine and good to

Provide for us as it should.

*dedicated to Travis Potts

1/3/06

Down for the count,

Beaten by my very own shame.

I raise my fingers from where

It was split.

Washed back by my saliva,

I try not to taste what may

Be washed down my throat—

Returned to be with what else

Might be digested.

I've never known shame like

This before—my enemy looming

Over me and laughing as he

Watches me die inside.

1/3/06

Sly,

You walked right by

Before I even had a

Chance to notice that

You came my way.

 Why do you insist on

Avoiding me, when you

Know that you cannot hide forever?

Hide from what you could

For such a solid opinion—

Something you could have

Given time to before you

Slipped away.

This time, I won't take

The blame; I have nothing else

To say.

1/3/06

Who would have thought that

You could make it into an

American night, so full of vice

That it would not

Take much time

To make a normal person's

Head spin?

You must be trying to get to

The same place where everyone

Else went some odd years

Before you were born.

You have no

Time to rumble

Before you mourn the loss of

What is going to be.

I cannot say that I agree,

Although I might not blame you

As I should.

If all for the good

Of the decency

Of your heart, with which

You did not find it hard to part.

Nothing could be this prearranged—

Deranged and stuck to some

Oral agreement like glue;

I do not envy you because all this

Is only a dream.

1/3/06

Slow, like you are trying to

Prolong the agony—like

The peeling away of new skin.

I knew that I should never

Have let you in for such

A formal display.

People should find that they

May get nervous around this

Time of day.

You do not fall in with the crowd,

Nor do you know how to turn off

The inner workings—so few and far between.

Come clean to reveal your source.

1/3/06

House full of flowers—

Like the coming of the spring day.

You thought wrong if you

Questioned that I had to get away.

I only want to get closer

To this source of happiness

And warmth because it's one

Of the things that brings me joy

In this shapeshifting world.

1/3/06

You want me to be all over it

With you so that we show

The world how we walk

When we get as down and dirty

As can be.

I had to find something exciting

And new so that you would

Not grow tired of my flower—

Our haven hot and sticky

With love that can be made

Thousands of times over again.

Tell me when you want to

Come on over back for more;

Knock on my door.

1/6/06

Random thoughts scattered

Across dimensions that are

Changed at any given time

To go with the majority of

Transportation.

Lesser thought will bring down

Any man that wishes to be

With any rational thought

Or description to change into

A piece of nothing, once all

The rambling is through;

Give me something new.

1/3/06

The edge of reason driven

From the brink of human insanity.

Who knows exactly why people

Do things like they do?

They think that life is an epic

That takes some getting used to,

As they want to be fulfilled

And given great opportunity,

As we open our mouths to

Talk and sing.

You needn't illustrate any

Points on this thing because

They can only make sense.

When you twist them a certain way;

Be all this as it may, I think I am

Safer right here…

1/3/06

I love the way you do these things

To stop me from feeling blue,

Like when you hold me and tell me

That our love can stop any pain that I

Have in this world.

You always know how to make

A smile appear on my face,

Despite the deepest frown

That took root there only hours before—

An amazing talent that only

One like yourself can have for the

Rest of our days, as we help each other

Survive in the eye of the storm.

*dedicated to Travis Potts

1/16/06

Call me when you need me,

Whether it's in the middle

Of the night or the prime of day.

You know that I will always

Be glad to see you though

To any place that you want to go,

Any place that you want to be,

Especially if it is with me.

I can take you there on my gilded wings

Whenever you call; remain with

A certain peace of mind because

I'll always have you as mine.

*dedicated to Travis Potts

1/16/06

Most of the time, I wish

You were the one person

Who I could see on a daily basis.

You're the one—the only one

Who can make time stand still

In its tracks—

The only one who can make

Everything else disappear

Within itself to make it remain

Outside of our lives.

To get lost in ourselves, only

To extract the finest meaning.

*dedicated to Travis Potts

1/16/06

Say what I want to do

Every moment of each day—

To hold you so dear

When everything else

Has already disappeared.

Your hand is the very key to

My warmth and happiness.

When I am most in need

Of consolation and escape

From this world, I feel

Secure knowing that I can

Take it anytime that I need,

While I tune out everything else

That tries to get my attention.

*dedicated to Travis Potts

1/16/06

Of all the things that I say I want,

You take your place at the

Top of the list.

You are the very essence that

Makes my soul radiate with warmth;

That's one thing that money

Cannot buy.

And that's one thing that time

Cannot replace, though some

Speak as if it could.

Number one priority that no

Monetary value could surpass

Or pay for with its earthly substance.

The human soul of one man is

Far worth more than its weight in gold.

*dedicated to Travis Potts

1/16/06

Typical exhaustion

Takes place almost all the

Live long day until I can

Hear your voice or feel your

Fond embrace.

Too much haste when I cannot

Partake of the sanctuary of

Your company, but when I

Return from the daily drudgery,

I can do nothing but run into your arms

And deflect all the harms that try

To make their way inside our

Sacred realm.

*dedicated to Travis Potts

1/16/06

When I feel the best

Is when I recall all the

Fine memories that we have

Together to feel glad in

Knowing all the things we can do.

When the two of us are together,

The world is ours, and there

Is no stopping anything that we

Can do or anything that we

Have planned because no one

Can meet our demands.

*dedicated to Travis Potts

1/16/06

Things like this never go

Out of style, especially since

We wish we could make another day

Just to share as lovers—just as the

World originally intended—to escape

The pressure and monotony of the

Everyday world.

A day in which we could hide

From all the others in the world

And pretend that we have one

Of our own.

If I could create an extra day

For the likes of you and I, then

It would be done with the snap

Of the fingers on a wishful whim.

*dedicated to Travis Potts

1/16/06

You know how to play on

The sympathies of those who

Think they are unsuspecting,

Though they know just what

They have done to you in less

Than a moment's notice.

Everyone knew, but they chose

To ignore the claims you made

Right in front of your face.

People like that just don't

Realize the emptiness that

Is most prominent when they

Are not looking—

Emptiness in their minds and souls,

As they find it hard to accept

Anything outside their shallow beliefs.

They think it's not their fault—

That the world finds itself so perplexed

With each new movement.

1/16/06

Last night befell a tragedy,

More than anyone would

Wish to know

Alas! Our angel

Was taken away,

Struck down in his

Young prime—

After we all

Had time to know

Him best and

Partake of the joy

That he brought,

Weeping through the hours

And trying to reach all the

Comfort we sought.

(Who would have thought) that

Such a tiny being could make

Our hearts tremble and enlarge

To less than

Three times their

Normal size.

Our baby,

Almost like a human

Child, like a little man who

Ensnared the world with all the

Great qualities he possessed.

Lest, he will never be forgotten…

*dedicated to Ashley—you will surely be missed

2/22/06

Epilogue

May you rest well, blessed in the heavens—

Having all you desired here on earth.

May we eventually come to feel glad

That we got to have you in our lives

Though we may find that we recover,

We know that we cannot fully get over

Your loss because you have given us so much

With your presence and great love as we know

That you are looking down from the heavens

Above and witnessing as we carry with our lives.

And we know that we should not bring ourselves to shame

Because we miss you all the same.

*dedicated to Ashley

2/22/06

Easy to figure out at such an age,

That I would lose the sense

Of security that I had when I was younger.

How can growing into my prime

Make me more vulnerable when it's

Supposed to make me feel more secure?

Your youth was different than mine—

A definition that does not always apply

(The same that one would think).

All I need is to get through these

Hard times that I thought I would never

Have to face.

Dependent, like I thought I would never be.

3/23/06

Visions of a sour future

Because I had such a great past.

Childhood so happy, how could

I have grown into such a sorry state,

And the bitter taste of venom won't

Leave me for anything, as I can taste

My own bile coming up through

My throat with the bitter imagery.

And all the words that I wrote,

What could have gone wrong;

Why have I failed?

I cannot answer these questions

In any great detail because I have

Nothing to say right now.

2/23/06

What did you think;

What did you want me to do

When you knew that I was

Going to lead you into some

Kind of trap?

 Like the teasing moment that

Sees me at my most invincible state,

So easy to do, yet you have not

Caught on.

No one ever does, and that is

What allows me to continue

Doing the things (I do) to perplex

And confound you with my

Every move.

It's what gets me off the most

In a world where you* all come out

On top.

*men

3/23/06

Whatever is said or done

Can determine the things that

Cross our mortal minds;

So scary, but reassuring

At the same time.

 We placed our bets on a dime,

And the world saw it as a crime,

And only you knew the difference.

You, who knew the most of all

The world and their mysterious ways—

Hoping that we could put a stop

To it all before we must put a stop to

Ourselves.

3/23/06

What I am or what I

Want to be—

So odd how they seem to

Have read my mind before

I was born.

How I lust and long for

The words to course through

My veins and mix through

My blood, until I can taste

It with my tongue!

A perfect representation of one

Mixed up human being, who

Wants to make it big in the world.

3/23/06

You do not remember me,

But I have been hiding in

The back of your mind for years

And hoping to resurface someday,

Bringing some kind of recollection

To what would have been if you

Had taken a different turn.

In this life, when everything

Seems so crystal clear, but nothing

Is exactly what it's supposed to be.

I would say you've got a hold of me,

But (it is I who's) I got a hold of you!

3/23/06

This is the tale of a sad woman,

Who had no life of which to speak.

Oh, if only one person would

Have made a difference, she would

Not have died in vain; she would

Have lived a life that could have

Rivaled the best (and beat others

By a long shot).

Alas! Nothing could have been

Further from the truth.

3/23/06

Go my way until you reach

The place where you grew up,

Where fond memories

Grow every day.

I can sing this over and relate

To it because they were all

With me, right by my side.

They laughed when I laughed,

And they cried when I cried.

Some could say that we were one

In the same, if I did not have

Such an aversion to the very idea.

But people will stick to their thoughts,

Just the same as I, though they cannot

Claim to have stronger memories

Because they have been recaptured

In the mind's eye.

3/23/06

I cannot help it—

This feeling that runs abundant

Through me at every point

Of the day.

Some have tried to tell me

That it would be this way,

But how it took me years to believe.

Though it was well worth the wait,

Everything else that was thrown my way;

I cannot say enough how

You make my every day!

Please stay where I can get a hold

Of you whenever I need some

Consolation.

3/24/06

Poor hearts

Stuck in opposition;

I did not know how to

Take what you were trying

To tell me, (and you) sell it

Like there is nothing other

To believe.

A normal part of life, and

I question its role in the

Healthy spot, where most

Relationships are supposed to be;

Set yourselves free!

3/24/06

How do you want to continue

Going on living in your

Current, sad state?

Something must be done to

Change back to the way

Things are supposed to be—away

From the everyday monotony.

 Think back to when you had a life

And before you were a wife,

Until a husband took it all away.

 Now you wish you were living

In another day so that you did

Not know this sorrow.

3/24/06

You took it all like the world

Came crashing down on

Your shoulders—

Alone like a child because

You are so young to have

To expose yourself to all

The sadness that can happen

In one's life.

So impossible because you

Were told that the world was

Supposed to work in a certain way,

And you don't have to listen to

Every word that they feel like

Planting in your mind—like the seed

That grows in place of tomorrow,

And all the dreams you once had.

3/24/06

The first time to open my ears

To something that has been

So close to me all along.

I can say how funny to note

The change and the color of my eyes.

Nothing more to despise or question,

Just confusion running rampant

In the heat of the night, and I must say

That I like it; I wouldn't have it

Any other way.

3/24/06

Are you trying to go in a

Different direction, that the world

Likes to turn its back on you?

Honky-tonk in an atmosphere

That is not familiar,

And the next thing you want to do

Is hightail it out of there,

Move on with your life.

3/24/06

Slowly, like a turning point

And a solid guarantee that

Things are going to be all right.

You have already turned yourself

Away from the dark night

That had you choking and gasping

For air.

What's only fair is something

That can measure an outcome

That will be favorable to us all.

3/24/06

Almost frightening how these

Ends come together, after

Hardly any kind of introduction at all.

I am far too familiar with the face down

Before the fall,

And I used to listen for the disturbing sounds

That vowed to echo inside my head.

 You swore that I would be dead if I wasn't

Moving my fingers.

Where fear lingers, in the most provincial

Place of all, you said you would be waiting

Near the shadows of the trees.

3/24/06

You happened to come to my aid

When I needed you more than I

Ever knew.

So much that my heart began to

Sing at a higher pitch, and I knew

Love in its greatest form with the

Beginnings that are so beautiful—

So have the idea that we can create more,

As we go along to further contribute

To a peaceful world in which we can

All coexist.

3/24/06

I hold your hand and embark

Upon a journey with you that

Will deliver us to the purest

Land of promise—the place where

We are destined to be and remain

Since the time of our creation, and

When we knew it, we left as soon

As we could, although much later

Than we should.

We have to see what's on other

Other side.

3/24/06

You've been through one year—

That best year of your life.

Now that you are husband and wife,

Things will appear as comfortable

As they have seemed for years

Through love, we can abolish

All the fears that plague our minds.

True love is defined by your actions,

Which shall last you the rest of your life.

3/27/06

So much has been done,

So many things have been said

Aside from all the thoughts of love

That swim around in your head.

And all that has brought you

Back to start a second year,

Which explains why your love,

In the first place, brought you here

Unexplainable, a phenomenon

In itself; did it take long for you to

Recognize all the beauty of your wealth?

And the metaphysics of love is sometimes

So hard to comprehend, but I know that

You'll have each other until the very end!

*dedicated to Chris and Shawna LoBue

3/31/06

I remember going to this place

Back in the day, when the sun would shine,

And people would gather to share their thoughts.

Collect them and show them off in this haven,

Where nothing would get in the way of what

People were trying to achieve.

Now I can hardly bring myself to believe

That such a place ever was and could

Have spread any kind of happiness to a human soul,

Anywhere on the vicinity of a planet, who is

Wrapped up in hedonistic involvement.

3/31/06

Last me through to the dawn

Of the day when the unacknowledged

Writer emerges from the shadow of doubt

And casts a mesmerizing spell on us all.

 I'm inclined to introduce him, but I'm

Not allowed to say what has made him want

To push in our way.

 Pressed for money—pressed for time in

A manner of speaking to make an appearance,

Then gracefully bow out to another habitat.

I know exactly where you are at and what

You want to see; all you need to do is follow me

To where the truth can evolve.

3/31/06

Why do you have to make it any more

Difficult on yourself, when you know what

I want stands right before me?

Don't make me beg on my knees to

Only further contribute to the disease.

I have to get what I crave,

Or else I may very well explode from

The passion I did not receive.

How cruel can you be to deceive me

When I need you the most?

Yearning inside and withering at the

Same time.

3/31/06

Fact of the universe

That you must hide your face

In the mud to get away from it all—

All the laughing faces that

Taunt your every move

From one point to the next.

Can one no longer be free?

3/31/06

Beginning to understand just

What you want from me—

This odd shell of a human being.

It's been months since you decided,

And you chose to take me in,

In spite of my idiosyncrasies.

Oh, now my love I will gladly give

Because you have rescued me

From obscene mediocrity

And sheer boredom that presents

Itself at a certain age.

One could say that it's not fair,

But I know that same old game,

And, this time, I came out on top.

3/31/06

Touch me until all the universes

Decide to collide and split up all

Of mankind.

In this fractured world, we can

Make all our promises come through,

And they will adhere like the strongest glue,

Which is meant to hold us all together.

3/31/06

Lucid liquid

Pounding to break

Our sweet tranquility

And further shame us

Into reducing our thoughts—

Making us think, like the

Insects we are.

I do not have far to go

To prove that I am not sane,

Like the way people would

Prefer to think.

Catch me in a drink, and whisk

Me away on a dream.

You are there to watch me

Stumble drunk into the next

Light, as I escape what I do not

Want to see.

3/31/06

I have discovered gold

In a foreign legion of such

A strange land; how long

Will it take for you to understand?

The instant dream of the situation—

When my words are not cracked up

To what they are all intended to be.

You claim you can see me,

Those loose thoughts that

Reside inside your head.

3/31/06

Swat team

Moving them in and out,

Though the voices are calling

Out at me to take a chance

To slow down.

They never knew what my life

Was really like, nor did they have

Any say as to how things were

Supposed to be—

Drowning in my own pool of blame

And human shame, what a waste;

What calamity has rung off inside

My head?

Do these people not even care who

They render dead?

3/31/06

Just to see how you work

And how you catch my eye,

As the day keeps wandering by,

And I am unaware of the night.

 Take me back to when I hardly

Had to speak, I was always good

At attracting attention (ever since my

Mind began).

So good a time that I always

Want to share my experiences

With anyone who cares to lend an ear.

3/31/06

I know how the song goes

And the word flows that are

Meant to be together, just as

A stem belongs to the rose.

Allow me to juxtapose (at this

Interval) to see what other

Phenomenon we summon.

4/2/06

You hear a story of a brave man,

Who sacrificed all for us and our will

To live as free Americans—

To go on with democracy for justice;

And the fallen will never again rise.

Who even knows or remembers

Such a man as he who gave what

Was rightfully his by God?

 No one that I can recall would fit such

A great description, or even match the

Inscription on their graves.

4/3/06

You give me anything but sweet

Simplicity, as I find it can sometimes

Take years to decipher your messages.

Received so many times over,

But quite often jumbled in with

Other things that have been lurking

For years.

Such a commonality; many could draw

Similarities like these, especially since

Not everyone can understand the same thing

At all times.

4/3/06

Better to know that I will

Be the one who can hold you close,

Anytime that something ominous threatens

To come our way.

You don't have to repeat what I say

With every word in my mind because

I know how to case your fear;

I know just how to love you, my dear.

Call upon me—talk to me with those

Sweet lips, I pray,

Any time of day because I would rather

Be with you than thrown into the faces

Of less than interested strangers.

4/3/06

Hard, pounding like you want to place

Yourself on top on top of me.

I could swear that I've died and

Gone to heaven.

Shallow? How could anyone twist

And manipulate the most beautiful

Thing that we have?

They do not have the right!

 No one has any of that insight,

Which makes us spectacular

In our own right, and all the world

Should be a flame!

Can't anyone follow the great example

That we have set for love?

And, every single metaphor seems to fit us

Like a glove, as we thrive to make

Our own record.

*dedicated to Travis Potts

4/3/06

Building my way up to a city

That could just as easily make

Me collapse.

Vice and sin are everywhere,

And how I want to wallow

In such a guilty air!

The phone will be off the hook,

As I separate the glistening,

White sands into neatly scraped lines.

Ingest, consume as much of this

Hedonistic moment so that

My head is nearly ready to explode,

Like the flaming

Beast within my heart!

Everyone doesn't have long until they

Get a start (at least what they want

To accomplish in their darkest hour).

 The mood has no time to grow sour

Because the endorphins do not need

Much time to kick in!

I am wallowing in every man's sin,

As I feel at the highest point in my life.

You did not know this,

But I have nothing

To confess, as I engage in every type of

Debauchery that exists.

Guilt has no hold on me here.

4/3/06

Epic of men, as they escape

And try to find something new.

Nomadic culture of the ancient times,

It makes me wonder how all the

Travel did not make them sick

To their stomachs.

4/3/06

Lament no more of the morose

Sadness that is stuck inside your throat

So that no sounds but sobs can escape.

We have finally arrived to the point

At which we want to be.

Time to bask in the sun and enjoy our

Well—deserved warmth;

It is here!

We can now pick up our feet that

Root over the winter and make

Our yearly progress, forward to the summer!

4/3/06

So lost and afraid in this place

That you hoped you would never find.

 Do not be inclined to have to turn

Away and break from the freedom of day.

Let yourself go and find someone who

Will help you find your way.

Purge your mind of these unwanted

Thoughts, so you can summon someone

To help you through.

4/3/06

That sound has been around

Since long before the creation

Of this being; who would have thought

That it would lead to much more

Than where it was intended to be.

For years, I have struggled with these

Burning questions in my mind.

Can you actually bring it upon yourself

To find any kind of reasoning that

Goes beyond the outer limit?

Something transcendental, yet equal

To matters of time and space—

Delighted to get lost in anything

Pertaining to reason and logic.

I follow anything that promises excitement

And stability to a

Life that has dedicated

So much thought.

To be human is to err, but to know that

We can learn from our imperfections can

Make us feel gladder.

Man should not know the terrible burden

Of being sad, and I should know what it's

Like to have billions of stars streaming by.

A simple quote to which a reply has been

On my mind, along with the cosmos.

Eventually, you will be shown the truth.

4/3/06

Laid back

In what you thought would be

A different kind of plan.

I have no idea what you are

Trying to say with all the

Different sound clips running

Through my mind—a Latino

Town turning into psychedelic paranoia

Before I even have time to turn my head;

You always knew how to play it right.

4/3/06

Get right back to it

Before my eyes start to close

(For the night).

All this puts me into such a

Tranquil mood, and it makes

Me feel as if the world has

Given me no difficulty, nothing

For me to worry about—

Just like back in the days

Before I existed, and the world

Was such a simple place.

No shame or disgrace can be

Mentioned when I am in such a

Complacent mood.

Food for my brain—can anything

Else remove me from my label

Of insanity, especially since I am in

An unconscious state of being?

My thoughts are still unseen…

4/3/06

I cannot let myself be held back

Any further; I've got to leave.

I've got to go where my body

Wants to stir—

Such a mental blur and a casualty

To modern fate.

I have a date with a destiny that

Will make me a new woman,

Complete with everything that I need.

Now I know that I will succeed

Because I have all my essentials.

4/3/06

Too cliché,

It would not do well for you

To be played in bars or places

Like a roadhouse.

Who would even know the

Greatness or remember the

Kind of things that it entails?

Too young a generation, and too old

To go back to where your mind

Relates to today.

It's so ironic; it cannot be said

Any better because people do not

Know if they are not in a certain loop.

I guess that's just the way things are.

4/3/06

Waiting in a place that I do

Not want to leave, but they are

Willing to hurl me out onto the

Streets, where the homeless

Find themselves asleep.

I cannot be one of them; I do not

Have the natural will to survive.

I want to stay inside, where things

Are relatively safe, and the people

Are allusive, in a nice sort of way.

 In here, I can do anything I want.

Out there, I am nothing of which to speak.

4/3/06

How do you feel about me,

After we've danced on the side

Of danger, and the white moonlight

Shone on our faces?

I'll never forget the time when you

Made a wild woman out of me.

One night fling; I think it happened

In the middle of the spring, while I was

Feeling a little unsure of myself.

Such a reassuring face (that was

Misconstrued for a mischievous smile).

I knew what it was like to dance on the

Other side once you introduced me to

The opposite of conventionality.

4/3/06

Inebriation

Of the finer souls

Happens to all of us

At one time or another,

Most likely when we are young

And plump with a youthful glow.

Our great memories flow,

Like the whisky through the barrels.

(Myself, I prefer wine.)

Just so long as we are able

To have a good time and remain

Sanguine in spirit.

4/4/06

Show those feet, legs pointed

High to march down the bloody

Streets of any town.

Sad will be the day when we decide

To make this a march

For victory—when the slain have

No choice but to lie in the streets.

Nothing more than rotting corpses,

Cheap pieces of meat of which to dispose.

When all of this starts to get out of hand,

And from the feel of it,

It seems that no one has noticed.

That's how shallow—how this

Town is when it doesn't come down

To the individual himself.

4/4/06

Fractured sky, how can you promise

To lead us to better days?

When all you know lies broken

With the rest of the sky, you cannot

Make such an outrageous claim.

You should know better than to feed

Us any more of your lies while trying

To disguise them as the beautiful truth.

No more liberating than the captivity

Of our souls—the blinding of our eyes;

False are the words that try to drag me

Into their sick realm.

4/4/06

You had to have seen that

I was afraid of any fast movements

Made by those on the other side

Of the field,

Like I am going to be the scapegoat

Or human sacrifice to some evil device.

Your menacing presence disturbs me

To say the least, and you have the

Nerve to ask what ails me.

Go away!

I can see right through you

And your heart of black,

And looking at it just

Summons up the courage to

Throw these ominous ideals back

In your face!

4/4/06

You take me halfway around the world,

Set sail on an extravagant vessel,

And I see sights that remind me

Of underwater paintings.

Explorations of villages, then I start to fade

Just before you try to reach down and

Place your lips on mine; I feel myself begin to

Lose consciousness before I am placed

On a bed of feathers.

4/4/06

Attraction to the slightest hint of distraction;

How I would love to reside in this kind of area

If, indeed, any exist.

I don't think that I shall be easy to miss (if anyone

Even knew I was there at all).

Everyone will know (that I have not gone) when I

Do not answer the call.

4/4/06

Average span two minutes;

That is how you feel when

You are in love—

 Like time is no object, and

Years seem to fly by in days.

And the beating of a heart can

Rage like a storm in the chest

Or be as tranquil and calm as

A whisper inside oneself.

And, in so little time, I can

Find myself renewed, just like

The plants that are revived in the spring.

4/4/06

Words by the man

Who were brought to the light

By his voice,

So beautiful that no other poet

I know can think of anything

To compare or measure in the

Human mind, though I would

Gladly claim it as my own.

Anyone would like to, and some

May have thought that it's already

Been done.

4/4/06

Do you really want to know

What goes on beyond my closed doors?

Can I see the faces staring in at me

Through the rain?

Eyes devouring my flesh—what is not

Left to the imagination.

Steam in the showers, and clothes

Piled on the floor, as I reach for my robe

And depart to the next room because

Nothing else may very well happen if no one

Is there to watch me get situated or begin

A new routine.

4/4/06

I want to get down,

Down, and raunchy with you

Now that my eyes have narrowed

And I'm in the mood.

So much to accomplish and so

Little time to waste.

No more haste, as we climb into

Action and give all the spectators

A show!

Go into the other room, where

I'll be waiting…

4/4/06

One snapshot, a frame inside

My mind.

Capture one, precious image,

Then the next.

The metaphor or infatuation

Lies within, then you can

Know how long this went on

And how it will continue to eternity,

Where there are infinite possibilities.

4/4/06

Measure the years between distance

And fears because we will always

Outnumber you as they one up us.

Never-ending through the legacy of man,

Then you find yourself on the wrong

Part of the cycle, though you did not

Wander there by choice.

No, the world is always about youth

In their prime, no age more or less—

Did you find it hard to confess when

You made the claim—that you wished it

Would have happened a lot sooner,

Like the collapsing of a tidal wave?

4/4/06

Resigned to sad silence and

The fact that the melancholy feeling

Will not go away.

I try to rid myself of it at the end

Of every day, but something so cruel

Lingers in my mind and prevents me

From thinking about all the sunshine therein.

One can never win with

Such a burden to bear;

This had made me think that others have

Felt the same kind of pain, but how can

Another individual relate just the same as I?

We all know what it's like to cry and to

Lower our heads to the ground, then you go

On some kind of mental rampage because

Your poor and tired mind does not have

The capacity to think rational thoughts.

Jilted, torn at the side, and the delirium has

You not knowing what to do.

You cannot count how many people

Have been through the same thing because

There are too many, and they all have

A different way of going through this mental

Breakdown until your reach the orgasmic point

Of losing total control, and only small remnants

Are found of you, waiting quietly in the background;

Now it is all over.

4/5/06

Sorrow in your time of need—

To watch a human heart bleed

In knowing that it has to struggle

For the will to survive.

Only a small part of me knows

How you truly feel because you have

Lost someone so dear, my thoughts

And prayers are near to provide you

Some comforting warmth until

You are able to pull through, slowly

At a time as you can.

Heal on your own speed, my darling,

Because you do not have to meet any demands—

Only to know that you are doing the best you can.

Time will eventually eliminate all the pain

That you are feeling inside; instill your

Faith in God!

4/5/06

Night's blue stars lead us

Along the wall, as we make a break

From the day, and dreams dance

Inside your head.

I never proposed anything

To make this pattern stop.

4/5/06

Fond Wishes for a Special Woman

A week of rest this time of year

Is cause for a celebration

And birthday cheer.

And, now, you can do what you please

With your assorted time, without

Having to answer any calls that are not

Pertaining to anything short of paradise.

Everything good you have earned

Will come your way, as you enjoy your stay

With a loved one.

Heaven on earth—savor every moment

That you can.

*dedicated to Amy Maddalon

4/5/06

1.2.3.4.5.6

Three seconds after two minutes

After 1:00, this is where I stand.

On April 5, 2006, another blink

And you'll miss its moment,

Another oddity that makes

People think, *How neat.*

How do you immortalize something

So small, but it may seem large to

Someone else—perhaps in another dimension,

Where things of this nature make sense

And rational explanations are few and

Far between, though it is something

That occupies my mind for a time

So that I can stay awake longer than

I should.

4/5/06

Woman form,

Entangled in the sheets,

Hidden under the covers

To make her feel like one

With the bed.

You can see life even after rest

And witness as she tries to

Blend in with her surroundings.

Nothing can ever break this dream,

So mellow and supreme.

Now I know that I can partake

In such great delight before

I turn out the light to lead to

Many happy tomorrows.

4/5/06

I suppose I'm the type who

Likes to run away, living just to

Get through another day.

Watch me hide in the corner,

In hopes that no one will

Notice me—that I'm not

Supposed to be there.

(I want to be) away from my

Designated post so that this

Part of the world may turn

Without me—the part that I

Don't know how much longer

I can take.

4/5/06

Stuck in neutral

To make a person drive

And shift his gears to

Those up and coming and

Make sure that he is still

In the running.

The race is on for the redemption

Of the prize.

Eyes wide inside his head

To show that the goal is far

From dead, quietly resting

In the recesses of his mind.

4/6/06

So quirky, I love the way you work,

So I am dedicating this silly verse

To you to portray my adoration for

Someone who is not afraid to be unusual.

Refreshing and endearing in a way;

I can sing this to you all day long…

4/6/06

You know where I stand with you,

And you're the same with me.

There is never a time that I do not

Want to be with you because you

Take the highest priority of any person

On this earth, and anyone can see

That I love you more than life itself!

Extend your arms to me and feel my

Warm embrace!

*dedicated to Travis Potts

4/6/06

Song of a man who's had enough

Of getting the run around that he

Should never have received.

Sometimes, it's just hard enough

Being in the mortal flesh, and on

Top of that having to deal with your

Emotions is not the easiest thing to do—

Just let the poor man go before his

Heart explodes.

4/6/06

I like to look out for you

Because you are my pride and joy.

One enamored being, this is

Worth seeing into the future

For the long run.

And, one day, we can look after

Each other, just as God has

Intended for us to do for eternity

To match.

*dedicated to Travis Potts

4/6/06

Falling into the rhythm

Of the strange notes placed in my head,

I can't help but tap my feet and follow

The beat of this weird substance

That took many hours to rehearse.

Someday, I may just find myself

Adjusting to all of this, though I never

Thought I would before.

There are so many things that still

Have yet to cross my mind.

4/6/06

A roller coaster of feelings,

Surely one will know that

Most of them are good—all of

Them when I get to be with you.

Ending days, how I long for them

When I am in your presence for any

Amount of time; you know that I am

Feeling fine when you are there

To shelter me in your arms.

And all the time, the drums of my heart

Are alive because I know that this love

Is the real thing, for sure!

*dedicated to Travis Potts

4/6/06

No words that I could speak,

No thoughts that I could think.

[I] have the capacity to describe our great love

And how you make my life complete, oh,

If I can only dedicate more of it you!

 If only the world didn't call,

(Especially if it's not all that pleased)

So that I could attend to your every need.

Thus, at least, making one more soul happy.

*dedicated to Travis Potts

4/6/06

Perfect Configuration

I have known it early on,

And I know you felt the same

Since whenever we began to speak.

Whatever has brought us together

Is much stronger than anything that

Could try to tear us apart!

We have made it so that our heart(s)

Cannot be denied anything that is

Implied with feelings of love.

*dedicated to Travis Potts

4/6/06

No more tales of your depressed childhood—

About how you tried to escape.

I have had it up to my ears,

And I feel like I may have even lived it

In the past life.

Although, I must at least say you have

A good attitude about how things could get better;

Not every soul can make such a claim to

Make his or her situation as good as that.

4/6/06

Not to be taken seriously;

I wish I could say that about

Everything I encounter—

(What I want to make things

Out to be).

Just take time to appreciate

The humor in life once you

Are guided to its doorway.

4/6/06

Change the tune with the

Snap of my fingers, to make

It go, faster or any way

That I please—

To possess that kind of power

Would be the best thing

I could have right now in

This shallow thinking, shallow

Is all it is, but I know that I need

A quick fix, sometimes, to get

Me going before all the heads

Start rolling.

4/6/06

Faces out of the cold rain

Do not remind me of the

Places I've been to in my youth,

But they make me want to

Take myself away from the heavy

Burden of man.

Someday, I will have dreamt it all;

How much longer will it be until

I have reached that point?

I don't want to (turn back and)

Say that all this thinking has been

Done in vain.

4/6/06

Hallucinations

Would be the only things

That would make me

Return to any destination.

That is a pleasant alternative

To this conscious state;

At least nothing could touch me there

And bring me down from my high,

Ever on the prize of never having

To feel the pain.

4/6/06

<hr>

Dilate transcendentalism

And the inner being that

Likes to grab you like the exotic,

Eastern sun.

4/6/06

Repeating the same words

After you've already run

Out of other things to say—

(I must admit that I have

Done so and to hatch new

Thoughts, each day is hard).

Subject to repeat fate unless

I undergo some kind of

Epiphany that allows me to

Make an analogy of my own.

4/6/06

Know where this is going,

Run the path through many times

In your mind, so that you may come back

Any time that you would like.

A secret place all laid outside in your head,

But you can only return if you have what

You need to get inside; this is not an

Entirely free ride.

4/6/06

You remember a time

When the weepy violins made

You think of a vintage scene

That cannot escape your mind.

For all that it's worth,

I trust I can hear whatever

I claim though, sometimes,

It runs out of my head.

You knew that I had a harder time

Understanding now that I am older,

But more youthful times will

Bring it all back.

4/6/06

Clever the way you try to

Fool millions with a popular parody—

A melody that so easily gets stuck

In our heads,

As if they could not know where

You came from to get anywhere

Further in an expression, not to

Mention that you have done it more

Than once, and we all know how people

Learn by reputation.

4/6/06

I do not have what you need,

So you feel that giving me

A swift kick in the rear

Will get me moving in one

Direction or another.

Scattered are the contents of my brain,

Which were thrown off guard by your blow.

Now, don't tell me that you can't see

The consequence of trying to make another (person)

Willing when they are perfectly content

Doing what they have been doing for years.

 You cannot break such a routine, especially

By force that is not yours with which to begin.

4/6/06

It has come upon us again

To express ourselves

In a physical manner—

Like the way nature originally

Intended for us to do.

I can tell by your face that

You have no objection to my plan

Because you want to do the same

As soon as possible.

Why hesitate, why give any wait

To what is being done all around us,

In this cesspool of raw emotion?

It is here and now that we should

Let our actions speak.

4/6/06

Wandering bard, so strange

To see you carry on, though

It is interesting all the same.

Do many people still know

That you're alive, doing

What you can to make it

Through another day or

Another week?

It is recognition that you seek,

And you seem to have come

To the right place.

Come to face the news—you

Can never bring him back, but

The spirit still lives on in what

You do today.

Who are you that you can say

There is nothing left to which

To look forward?

4/8/06

Get moving nearly as fast

As you can to get to know

Something that has gone astray,

But maybe you tried to capture it

Sometime before.

Don't think of it as a never-ending chore

Because you will go nowhere that way.

You should have more say in what you

Want to do, but you've got to make

An effort to see what you need to

Get accomplished with your speed.

4/8/06

Different beat

That wants to carry me

Farther east,

When the rest of you

Turn your backs to avoid

Any conflict that could

Blow up between us.

Not wanting that to happen—

Confused still on where to go.

The direction of the flow seems

Much harder when you don't know

How to navigate.

You can't be late to get to the

Only place you have to go.

4/8/06

Go inside

To grab a hold of what you need;

Now we must all begin to feed off

Raw energy that is fueled by your hand.

 Take my words the other way instead

Of having to analyze every, small piece

That finds its way to the highest part

Of your mind.

That's all you need to do.

4/8/06

The largest piece

(Of the puzzle)

Does not have to

Fit the best

Under the circumstance

That you come to find yourself

In the company of people who

Ask, "What are you going to do?"

And you find that you can only

Return a blank stare in the general

Direction of those who seem to

Have no clue, just as you.

4/8/06

On such a night

When you find yourself

Bored out of your mind

In this forsaken town,

Loneliness can be your enemy,

So you resort to substance,

Wishing you had some

Kind of human relationship

Of a carnal nature!

You're tired, and you just

Want to sleep it off, rather than

Having the will to change

Your mind for the better.

Sad case, what are you going to do?

Now that nothing can seem to

Save you from whatever the

Situation seems to be.

4/8/06

Imagine

Something that could be

So crystal clear—

Like the notes on a piano

Going with the flow of

The rest of the music,

Until then you hear

A human voice that rings

Out and sings a tale that

Relates to your life.

See the beauty of the freedom

That twinkles with the

Light in your eye.

  You no longer have to see me cry

Because this person has made it

So that everything will be fine.

In the heart of the music,

Whether it's played

By instruments or

Sung by the voice

Of the man who has lived

For so many years compared to I.

He has found something to

Make him want to continue

To another great place.

All my memories will not

Be erased.

4/10/06

Jumping into the scene,

To the beat of a tambourine.

You hear me go, and then,

Turn to face another direction.

I see that we have come

To an agreement about what

We want to see and what

We want to do

Through the things that

Have made us individuals.

We've had our share of

Similarities.

We've had the will to find ourselves

Climb to a great happiness that

Grows very intense at times, but it

Makes us glad all the same.

No longer facing despair and shame,

We know the very reason for the

Existence of such things as

They watch us grow into our new freedom.

4/10/06

Take back what you just said,

Before thoughts of vengeance

Fill my head and remove me

Completely detached from everything

That lives above the ground.

Don't make another sound until

I can feel the movement stirring

Within a close proximity of my

Vanished dreams.

4/10/06

I hear you in my mind,

And I wish that I could come

Your way to brighten up our day.

All the happiness you have given me—

All the choices for our love.

When I am with you, I feel most

Peaceful, and everything else in the world

Can wait because I am by your side.

When nothing can tear us apart

All I have to do is look into my heart,

Where I find you patiently waiting

For me to come look you up

And make both parts of our day.

I am glad you decided to come my way

And make my life the best that it can be.

*dedicated to Travis Potts

4/10/06

The skies look calm

And give us reason to find

Everything inside to bring it

Out of the world.

You know how much I like

To dream and how much

I say that

I need you in

My life, forever.

I've got to have you so that

I can live knowing

That our love

Is something so great.

 Everyone who has felt love

Should be able to relate

And want to join in to have

A chance at it themselves.

And the greatest

Joy of their lives

Will unfold before

Their very eyes.

  So easy to recognize now that

I have you!

*dedicated to Travis Potts

4/10/06

You took the best dreams

And made them into a reality

So that my life will be lived

With such happiness that I

Never thought such a mere mortal

Could know.

Very soon, I will know which way to go,

According to what I like to see.

All this happiness is beaming inside of me,

So much that the world has to know

Because there is no other choice.

My voice, because of you, will finally

Be heard with the great difference

That you have made because you are

The one who has made my life shine!

*dedicated to Travis Potts

4/12/06

Once a society written

And compared has seen me—

Fully prepared in having the knowledge

Of what to do when I am not quite through.

Glowing with recognition and personal stance;

(I am) delighted to have this chance to

Break through all my boundaries.

4/12/06

Palm Sunday

In one more week,

Our Lord will rise

And tell us that

He will come to save us all,

That the debt has been paid,

And we may ask forgiveness

Through Him.

The greatest thing to happen,

The greatest story ever

Told throughout the years—

The Lord will eliminate our fears

And set us free so that

We can love just as we are

Intended to do.

Spread the message, make peace—

Do what your mortal vessels may

So that the world may know of His

Unconditional love and sacrificing action,

Which has allowed us to live forever

In the kingdom of heaven—to know

The God Who created us in His image

And given us all an option of paradise

As His best-loved creations.

And we are to carry on His name

And the message of peace to mankind—

To help each other as we try not

To fall into the sin that would

Trap us forever.

We shall help each other try to

Find the light, as it is given to us

By the Messiah and spread throughout

Our hearts!

4/9/06

I wish you much success

And happiness on this day,

When you play a great part

Of sharing God's love.

Today, like all days, you

Have loved ones surrounding,

Cheering you on as you tell

Us a story and send us a

Message of peace.

God has blessed His house

And given you an audience

As you take center stage

To play the part of the

Greatest Man who ever lived,

And we are all glad to know

That you did because you know

How to spread the story of our Savior.

*dedicated to Greg Smith

4/8/06

What I have seen in between

Comes to take on a different meaning

When all the outside focus

Starts to shift in.

Watch all the greatness begin,

As I find something worth

Climbing up to and obtaining

Someplace near here or in my dreams.

Suffice to say, my third eye is watching.

4/8/06

Death inside,

I almost cried

And tore out every last

Strand of my hair.

You stop and stare, then

Only point a finger

In my direction.

Bony and accusing,

You knew that I had

To get a brand in my skin

To move.

What do you have to prove

After such a long day of

Tedious labor?

Nothing left to

Thrill and savor,

As every taste

Has run bitter

On my tongue,

And if it were

Even lighter and warmer,

I would

Run to the nearest place and disappear

From you all once the new blood settles in

To take me away.

3/25/06

White plague death,

What does the world see

When mixed with red-pink, hardly

A stabilized color, so new to

The human eye?

Imagine stretching out beyond

Your normal bounds to match

The coldness of the night.

1/17/06

I want to keep you impressed,

Keep you intrigued with a fascination

That comes along with me.

Captivate your imagination

In the wake of the moment—in the

Spectacle of the blinking eye.

I'm more than an infatuation;

I'm a dream.

Obtainable by any means and

Any circumstance—not the

Unrequited love that many would think

Me to be and rue the day that I came

Into existence, at least for you.

I'm the good kind with whom you

Would like to have an affair, as you

Watch me standing there (by your side).

1/17/06

Drowning in my own sea of remorse,

With no one else to blame or thank, (of course).

Expendable human being, whose mortality

Stays on a threatening, unsteady brow.

Exasperated sigh, these days

Have to only run a certain way,

Which is not in my favor.

1/17/06

I can't take this aggravation

Only to end up in eternal damnation—

One year of hell, while my life

Slowly falls apart.

What have I done, what can I do

To make it so that all these bad things

Can disappear?

As I look back on this year and

Realize what a fool I already am—

Then I hate myself for having to breathe,

I hate myself for having to live.

You can get the idea, although

You may not understand because you

Have been trained from the start.

You like this kind of docile life of

Servitude when everyone else is around,

But what really happens when the lights

Go out inside your head?

The grace of God is the only thing that

Has allowed me here today.

1/17/06

Pour all the bad thoughts

Down the drain while I

Keep myself from

Going insane and harming me

Further, while a speculating crowd gathers.

You knew those kinds of people

Who have a morbid curiosity about pain.

With that kind of attitude, you have

Nothing to gain.

2/21/06

Instant shovel down

My barely receptive throat.

I've failed her*, I've failed life,

I've failed myself.

How much sooner can my

Weary eyes receive a rest;

When can I finally prove to the world

That I am not the best?

I hate to be here—hate it so much

More than those who already know

That they are perfect (or close to it).

Don't they have their own lives;

Don't they realize that I want mine

And that I try to do my best dressed in

These business suits?

I try, I smile, and I greet, knowing

Full well that they won't remember

The next day; sometimes it doesn't matter,

Anyway.

Long and unwinding this road seems to be

Now that I have to contend with technology,

And it will only get worse as the years go by.

Sometimes, I don't know whether to laugh or cry

Through this foolish, mortal blood while I wish

That I could remain unseen after I've done

Any wrong.

To safely sleep in some kind of corner—

Will no one know when to stop looking for me?

*Sylvia Plath

2/21/06

Serious, My Love

You've opened up doors for me,

And it is because of you that I can breathe.

I have no need to grieve or think

Lesser thoughts because of the intellectual

Freedom that is present; you challenge my mind.

Oh! Not a simpleton can see anything of the sort,

Great genius; you make my every day because

I know that you are my equal.

(This is) the most serious love that I have felt,

So much so that I never want to leave.

You know you can believe that my heart

Beats true colors for you.

All the time echoing

Your name in my head

With such extraordinary thoughts that

Most outsiders cannot even begin to fathom.

I could not think of such things before,

When my mind related

To thoughts so hedonistic,

But you removed me from such a sad state.

  You have helped me eliminate thoughts of hate—

Now vanished from my mind.

The sign, and you are a true gift from God

As long as I am able to cherish anything,

You will be on top of my list.

*dedicated to Travis Potts

3/7/06

So many things to say

For all you mean to me.

My thoughts want so much

To connect with what I

Wish to tell.

Months I have known you,

Though it seems like years,

In only the best of ways.

I look forward to the many

Days ahead of which we have to spend—

So many things in life to share,

Such as the blessing through a new

Love that has bloomed—such is the

Blessing of having gotten to know you!

*dedicated to Margie Potts

3/4/06

…And those you love

Will be quick to say

That you can brighten up the world

In your own splendid way.

A talent all your own

To cherish the space in which

You have grown—

 To live according to your heart.

In presenting thoughts to share;

We all know just how much you care.

*dedicated to June Hendershot

3/4/06

Two more days left,

Pent up in a hotel room.

No mistaking grimness

From the total gloom.

Now don't you say that's OK

Because you knew just what

I meant when I said that this

Was an accident.

 Look at me as I hold my

Teeth clenched tight, like I'm

Trying to erase myself from

A dirty fight.

 Early morning, now I wonder where

The hell you went.

And I'll search all over now—

 Search all over now until

I track you down in your path.

3/15/06

Contemplating Fame

  Not so young it happened,

But it happened all the same.

Once opened up

The door to fame

And saw a shining light

Beckoning from the other side.

 To think that

I actually confided

In myself enough to allow this

Change of events.

(Repent)

I have not done

Much in the way

Of sin—especially step on any toes

Just to see the tears of pain.

Not so much of a loss as a regain

Of what I think I have deserved

Over the years, though it must

Take me a while

To get over my fears

Of a large crowd

That could potentially

Swallow me whole.

 I have to purify my soul if I want all

These good things to come to me.

3/29/06

Adulation

Once the crowd looked up at me
And cheered my name, I knew
That I did something worthy of praise.
I haven't felt this much pride in days,
(Years if you would like to ask).
Lo and behold, I saw my name
In sparkling lights, as they carried me
Away from the field to a place where
I could be taken care of, where no more
Thoughts of sadness could cross my head.
Now we all be jovial instead of having to
Admit that I thought nothing would
Become of me before—as if I'd just
Shut the door.
Could this be a second calling, something
New to get me started and make me
Feel good about myself, as if to know that
I have accomplished something that
Makes me worth the while.
Now my life shall not be lived

In vain as I hear my name echoed

Through the stands and, for the moment,

I can do away with the humility that is

Supposed to always be at my side, just

So long that my head does not fill with

Too much pride!

3/20/06

Vernal Equinox

Today marks the end of the curse

And welcomes the beginning of spring,

When we can now have a fling with

The outside world, and our senses

Can reawaken to man.

Stand an egg upright during the

Middle of the day, and test the theory

That is known all around the world.

I do not know when I get to see such

A splendid myth in the making,

But I know that this thing shall stand

As a sigh of relief in most rites,

And it will help me get through the nights.

3/20/06

Wishes for Success

I know you will do well,
On this day of days, because
Opportunity belongs to you and
All the progress
That you made.
I know you shall make us proud
With victory at your side,
And the world
Will know what
A great man you are.
Searched by so many month
With me by your side, and
I am so glad
That I can be here
To witness your
Time to shine.
Here in love and spirit, and
Through God, of course you know
That you do not
Have to go through

This alone,

Especially because of the

Persistence you have shown.

This day, you will show them just

What you are made of!

*dedicated to Travis Potts

3/21/06

I wish that could stay warm

And well in your familiar comforts,

Instead of having to go outside

And face the day.

How I wish that I do not have

To fight the elements that should

Not even be here at this time of year.

 Full gear, sweet dreams *mostly*

Come best when my eyes are

Tightly closed, and my body fully warm

From the embryonic comforts we knew

Before we had to go out and make our way.

(Not to say that I completely dislike it),

But I would rather be here with my love

So that we can thrive and bask in

Each other's warmth instead of being

Forced upon the world's plate

(For consumption).

3/21/06

Why does childhood matter

So much when most don't

Really care how the other half lives?

Youth is a secret that everyone

Would like to keep, but it disappears

With the wind when you reach the

Point at which it gets harder

To conceal all the fine lines.

And what about the elderly, do we

Have no more respect for them than

We do for than the dead?

Early graves vandalized by our

Sharp words.

Sometimes, we have no shame.

3/22/06

Whiskey rebellion

In a slightly modern time,

And the man just chugs

Them down, like there's

Nothing else to do.

World on his shoulders;

This is his way of making a

Decision with the flick of the wrist.

Sometimes, it may have went unnoticed,

But he no longer thinks with his

Poetic mind—now it's just all

Unintelligible syllables that come

Out between drunken slurs.

 Some say he might have been trying to

Deprive the world of his talent,

While others may not have an idea

What it means.

Those are the type who constantly

Have their eyes bloodshot,

And their breath reeks of abomination

(So sad, but true).

You had better get back to your former self

To reveal what you have to those who are

Still willing to listen.

The sensitive genius has to penetrate

Back into your head while you toss

Out the negative images that you

Cannot work around.

So little cannot be so late during this time

Because of the issue resolved.

I supposed you tried, you did try in

Your own way.

No more ill should be said.

3/22/06

To you on such a special day,

When words cannot describe

Just how much you mean to.

Those who love you, especially

When they take the time to

Celebrate and commemorate.

A day that marks a milestone—

This day when you were born

Is known by all those around.

And it is because of you that

Some of them had an opportunity

At life.

Then we go further to describe

How you have given so much

Over the years, so much so that now

It's your time to receive happiness,

In every sense of the word.

3/23/06

I can't help but wish you happiness

And everything else that comes

Along on this day because you deserve

It, as every hard working soul

Deserves a rest.

I can attest to such things because

I have seen you helping us out

And making us feel at home.

Such kindness shown cannot go

Unrewarded, especially for a person

Who puts forth great effort to do

What she does.

3/24/06

Enthralled by everything you have said

As thoughts of sweet love fill my head.

Life, the universe, and everything surrounding

Hold true the meaning when I think of you

And all the things we can do.

We are in love, and no one can deny

The privilege as it is related to man; I will

Always be your biggest fan.

Despite the fact that there are still cynics

In the world; we have the power to cancel

Out it all, lest we have something that will never

Allow us to fall.

(I'm) so fortunate to be

With you because it

Has given me another great purpose in life,

And I will someday be

Glad to be called your wife.

Oh, but for now, I am just glad to be your darling love,

Who cannot resist all your great charm, because

You have so much wonder to give.

So abundant that I would

Like to relive every moment.

Every sweet word you have to say will surely

Come my way because

The power of love, our love,

Is the greatest power by

Which we can live.

*dedicated to Travis Potts

3/24/06

Let me try again to capture this

With my words—this thing that

Has captivated me for the last six months.

I have told you a countless number of times

Just how much you mean to me and

How this vessel could not sail without you

And the great role that you play in my life.

I could not speak words that are truer

Because they circulate with the blood

That is pumped by my heart, which beats

At an accelerated rate every time that

I am in your presence.

It's a wonder that I haven't already felt

It explode, like everything else that comes

Into contact with you—that gets mixed in

With the rest of the feelings that we feel.

Oh, what it means to be young and in love,

Every poet's dream—everything that

Every song plays out loud.

Now, I no longer have to fear the loneliness

That would ordinarily haunt me because

I have emerged strong and hopeful of the

Promises that are going to ensure my life

Will be grand.

I get to know this as soon as you take hold

Of my hand and create the richest dreams,

Soon to become a reality.

*dedicated to Travis Potts

3/24/06

Careful acting for the rest of the day;

I don't want to lose my say and

Watch everything I have trickle

Down my fingers.

In such a cold state, my mind lingers,

As it wants to be set free, but I have

To play the part so that I can relieve my heart

Of the anxiety building up inside.

(These things) coincide to bring me happiness

In the end.

3/25/06

I am no stranger to the

Light fingers tapping on my skin.

To go with the moistening of the rain—

To have such cold at this time of year

Is enough to drive me insane.

Whatever happened to global warming?

I've all this energy bundled up inside,

And my slothful state is enough to hurt

Anyone's pride, as I witness these parts

Of my life go by.

Why can't everything go back to the way

It was, instead of being frozen just like

My poor counterparts of nature?

 So unreasonably cold—too soon come

Out of hibernation, and the trees have

Yet to grow back their beautiful leaves.

Why couldn't this death all have happened

Days sooner?

I am not too fond of dying.

3/25/06

Big Mark

Made in such ink that

Cannot be removed, I see

Such beauty traced on

Every part of the living land.

I cannot stand to see all of

These things go to waste.

This rich environment does not

Have much to be desired

Because everything I need is

Right here in front of me,

Where I can make an X

So large that no one can possibly

Miss the target almost meant

To be a bull's eye that creativity

Can strike after it finds me waiting

Right there, beside the big, red circle.

3/25/06

So much you expected to do or say,

Right before I was in the midst of

Getting my way.

No matter, I am leaving now to watch

You practically come apart at the seems,

While you cry uncontrollably and

Wish you had me back, but that

Cannot happen, will not happen, now that

I have found the one who will come to me

And make me happy to know that I can now do

And say—come and go as I please;

I'm no longer yours to appease.

4/13/06

A tooth has many parts,

Like a reptile has four hearts.

And many are glad to say

That they use them every day.

1991

*This is the first poem I had ever written. I was twelve years old, and the poem was part of my sixth grade science in-class assignment. (The first two lines came from memory, but I had to make up the last two.) I was the first to read my "work" because I was eager to share it with the rest of the class. Even then, I had the urge to present my poetry out loud. Needless to say, however, I have gradually refined my technique since then.

-Jen Selinsky

4/13/06

About the Author

Jen Selinsky was born in 1978 in Pittsburgh, PA. She was raised in Cranberry Township. In December 2004, Jen earned her MLS from Clarion University of Pennsylvania. She now lives in Sellersburg, IN.

Some of Jen's short works have been published in several anthologies, including *The Raider Review*, *Tobeco*, and *Essence of a Dream*, published by The National Library of Poetry—for which two of her poems, "Ode to the Forest" and "Realization," won an editor's choice award. One of her works was also recently published in *The Poetry Review.com*.